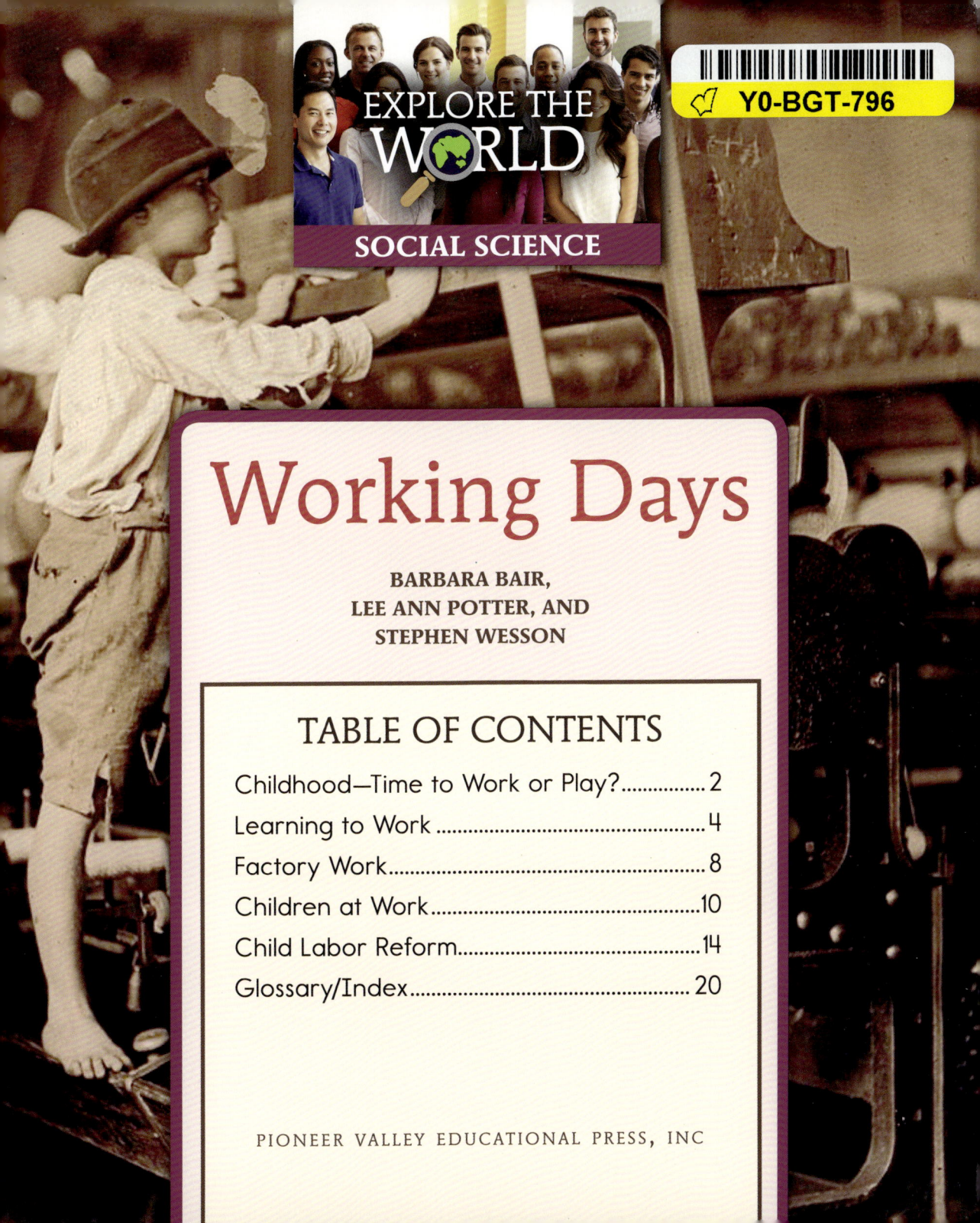

EXPLORE THE WORLD
SOCIAL SCIENCE

Working Days

**BARBARA BAIR,
LEE ANN POTTER, AND
STEPHEN WESSON**

TABLE OF CONTENTS

Childhood—Time to Work or Play?	2
Learning to Work	4
Factory Work	8
Children at Work	10
Child Labor Reform	14
Glossary/Index	20

PIONEER VALLEY EDUCATIONAL PRESS, INC

CHILDHOOD—TIME TO WORK OR PLAY?

"Childhood should be a time for young people to be **nurtured** and allowed to play and learn."

"Childhood should be a time for young people to work to keep them out of trouble and to build character and discipline."

Which of the two quotes to the left sounds better to you? Long ago, children did not have much choice in the matter. The idea that childhood should be a time of freedom and play is fairly new. Until recently, most American children spent their days hard at work.

LEARNING TO WORK

When people from Europe first came to America, their children had no choice of how to spend their time. They worked to survive. Even the youngest children had chores. They gathered wood, collected eggs, or pulled weeds in the garden.

Around age 10, a child might become an **apprentice**. Apprentices lived and trained with a grown-up who was an expert at their job, like a tailor, a baker, or a **sawyer**.

4

Long ago, a craftsman might have taken on an apprentice to have extra help in the workshop.

Girls at that time were not expected to work outside of the home, but some of them learned to sew and became hatmakers or seamstresses.

Some children without a family became **indentured** servants. They were often not paid, but they were given food and a place to live in exchange for their work.

Some children became slaves. They did work similar to indentured servants, but their lives were more difficult. Indentured servants were seen as people, while slaves were seen as someone's property. Some started working when they were only four years old.

Slave children from New Orleans.

7

FACTORY WORK

Long ago, things such as clothing and toys were made by hand. But by the mid-1800s, machines in factories were making these items faster and for less money. Cities began to fill with factories, and people moved there to find jobs.

Many immigrants from other countries moved to the United States to find jobs. Between 1890 and 1910, more than 11 million immigrants arrived in the United States. Most of them moved into crowded city neighborhoods and worked in nearby factories.

>>> **Factories exposed workers to dangerous levels of air pollution.**

CHILDREN AT WORK

The factories needed a lot of workers, and children were the cheapest workers who could be found. But places like factories and coal mines were very dangerous. The dust made people very sick. The high-speed machines put children at risk of accidents. At factories where food was packaged into cans, children could get scrapes and infections. Children worked in glass factories where they often got cuts, burns, and other injuries.

Some places that hired child workers were called sweatshops. Children working in sweatshops were crowded together in areas with bad air and no sunlight.

MORE TO EXPLORE

Workers in coal mines were surrounded by **HEAVY, THICK DUST**. The dust got in their lungs and made it hard for them to breathe.

Young girls who were not old enough to work in sweatshops might be hired to clean people's houses. Young boys often delivered newspapers or shined shoes.

Outside of cities, children worked in the fields, planting and gathering crops. This work was seen as more important than going to school.

In 1880, more than 1 million American children under the age of 16 had a job—that's one out of every six children at the time. And that's not counting the children who worked from home, making little objects to sell. They might sew clothes, roll cigars, or make toys. Families were paid for each item they made. Even the youngest children were expected to help pay the bills.

The three oldest children in this picture are Joseph (14 years old), Rosie (7 years old), and Andrew (10 years old). All three of them helped their mother to sew clothes. The family made about two dollars a week if they had enough work.

CHILD LABOR REFORM

Between 1890 and 1920, the laws began to change for child workers. There were people called **reformers** who felt that the government should do more to protect children.

Reformers supported laws that fixed the dangerous conditions facing child workers. They also helped to create more public parks and schools.

Jane Addams was a reformer who founded Hull House, a center that provided care and support for families with young children.

Kindergarten became common across the country because of these reformers. They also created after-school and day care programs for the children of working mothers.

Around this time, states began to pass laws requiring children to attend school at least part of the time. Sending children to school was a good way to make sure that they weren't being forced to work.

MORE TO EXPLORE

Some working **FAMILIES OPPOSED** the efforts of reformers because parents needed the money that their children earned.

Reformers made posters to gather support for their campaigns.

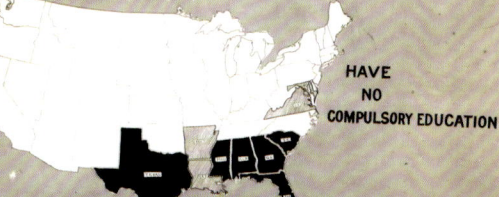

The National Child Labor Committee (NCLC) formed in 1904. This group helped bring about change for child workers. The NCLC improved workplaces and limited the number of hours that children were allowed to work.

Today, there are laws in the United States to protect children and give them a chance to play and learn as they grow up.

When the bell rings at 7 o'clock, we stop work. We hurry back to the boardinghouse, eat breakfast, and then it's back to the factory by 7:30. We do it all again for our noon dinner. After that, I am at my machines until closing time at 7 o'clock in the evening. We make our way home in the dark.

By then we are all so tired, we're ready to drop. Last night at supper, little Mary fell asleep right at the table!

Mama, enclosed you will find my first month's wages. I earned 14 dollars. They took out 5 dollars for my room and board, and I kept 50 cents for myself as you told me to. I hope the 8 dollars and a half will help.

I write this after church. I know you will be pleased to hear that we all follow the company rule and attend every Sunday. It is our only day off.

Your loving Grace

GLOSSARY

apprentice
a person who learns a job or skill by working for someone who is experienced at that job or skill

indentured
required by a contract to work for a certain period of time

nurtured
helped to grow

reformers
people who work to change and improve society

sawyer
a person employed in sawing wood

INDEX

accidents 10
after-school programs 16
American 3, 12
apprentice 4–5
campaigns 17
cans 10
character 2
childhood 2–3
coal mines 10, 11
craftsman 5
day care 16
dust 10–11
Europe 4
expert 4
factory 8–10
freedom 3
government 14
Hull House 15
immigrants 8
indentured 6
infections 10
Jane Addams 15
kindergarten 16
laws 14, 16, 18
lungs 11
National Child Labor Committee (NCLC) 18
nurtured 2
pollution 9
property 6
reformers 14–17
sawyer 4
school 12, 14, 16
seamstresses 6
slaves 6–7
states 16
survive 4
sweatshops 10, 12
United States 8, 18
workshop 5

20

A Letter from a Mill Girl

Dear mama,

Forgive me for not writing sooner. This is the first chance I have had.

I don't mean to complain, but—oh! my fingers are sore and my feet are so swollen. Let me tell you about my days. At 4:30 in the morning, the factory tower bell wakes us with a loud clanging. Such a scrambling goes on in our room. We must all be dressed and at the factory by 5 o'clock sharp or risk being locked out and losing our day's wages.

In the spinning room are rows and rows of big machines with huge, leather driving belts, all running at top speeds. You have never heard such a terrible, loud clatter in all your life. We have to holler to hear each other talk. It never lets up all day long.

All the windows are shut tight. It's so stuffy—a fine cotton dust flies everywhere. It makes me sneeze and gets in my hair something awful. It gets hot too. By the end of the shift, my dress is all wet down the back.

My job is to tend the spinning machines that wind thread onto rows and rows of tall bobbins. I tend eight sides. One side includes long rows of many bobbins, and you'd be amazed at how fast they spin! All day, I walk up and down on the lookout for broken threads. I must tie them together quickly so as not to stop the machine too long. The overseer keeps a sharp eye on all of us.